Secular Soulmates

The depth of their friendship
seeped into the next generation.

Hanif Mike Karim

authorHOUSE®

AuthorHouse™
1663 Liberty Drive
Bloomington, IN 47403
www.authorhouse.com
Phone: 1 (800) 839-8640

Published by AuthorHouse 09/16/2019

ISBN: 978-1-7283-1838-7 (sc)
ISBN: 978-1-7283-1836-3 (hc)
ISBN: 978-1-7283-1837-0 (e)

Library of Congress Control Number: 2019909032

Print information available on the last page.

This book is printed on acid-free paper.

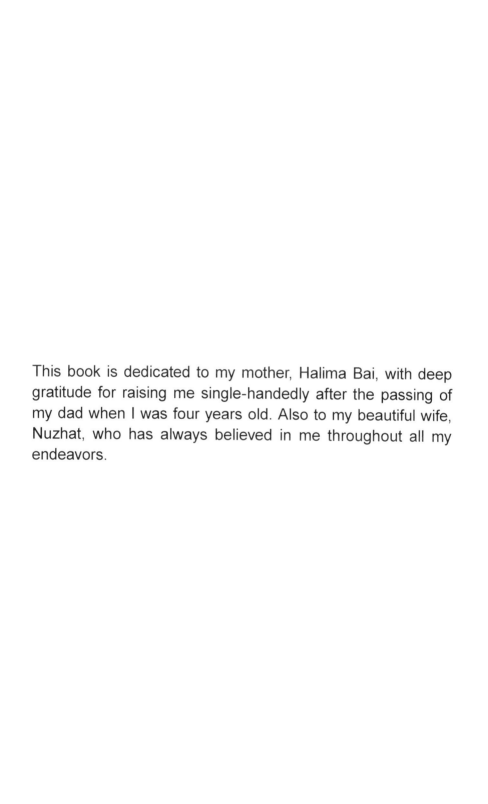

This book is dedicated to my mother, Halima Bai, with deep gratitude for raising me single-handedly after the passing of my dad when I was four years old. Also to my beautiful wife, Nuzhat, who has always believed in me throughout all my endeavors.

Contents

We all seek romantic love, as we are taught that a soulmate is someone we all need for our lives to be complete.

But it's the platonic love that really keeps us going through this quest of love and heartbreaks and everything in between.

Friendships are the most important relationships one can have—it's the ultimate form of accepting another human being into our lives.

It's the reason so many of us believe that being friends with your family and your partner is vital for the relationship to work.

Which is why we must do everything to cherish and nurture healthy relationships in our lives.

—Madhavi Pothukuchi

Characters

Ashok	Salim's son
Dilip	Shagufta's husband
Dr. Goldberg	Salim's doctor in New York
Manesh	Anul's daughter
Maryam	Anul's cook
Mr. Bhagwan	Ashok's lawyer
Mr. Desai	Manesh's lawyer
Mr. Dharmender	Manesh's family friend
Mr. Sharma	banker
Mustafa	Anul's driver
Shagufta	Salim's ex-girlfriend
Venu	Shagufta's driver
Anul Shetty	Salim's soulmate
Dr. Khanna	Salim's doctor in India
Judge	judge
Roberta	Ashok's housekeeper
Salim Sultan	Anul's soulmate

1

Saint Patrick High School had been in existence since before India's independence from Britain. It was built in 1928 under the direct supervision of Father Joseph Solomon. Father Solomon had promised his mother at her deathbed that he would build a school in her memory. His son, Mr. Antonio, took over after Father Solomon's death in 1971. The school had been run by the same family to this day. Currently, the principal was Mr. Anthony Davis, a distant cousin of Mr. Antonio.

For decades, the school had an ongoing tradition of organizing a yearly reunion of its alumni and students who had attended Saint Patrick's High at one time or another. They loved coming to this party from all over India and looked forward to it each year.

This year's reunion was no different. The venue was a huge playground with colorful shamianas (tents), food vendors, a decorated stage for introductions, special guests, and musical events. Big, round tables and chairs were set up throughout the playground for this festive, joyous occasion.

One such table was occupied by a distinguished-looking man, Anul Shetty. Sitting next to him was his daughter, Manesh, wearing a nice modern sari. There were some other guests sitting at the same table. People at the table mostly talked with those whom they already knew. One man at this table, Salim Sultan, sat alone. Although he was alone, he seemed to be thoroughly enjoying the occasion.

One of the traditions at this school reunion was to announce the names of the attendees and the year they'd graduated. That person would then stand up for a few seconds and be acknowledged.

When Anul Shetty's name and his year of graduation (1962) was announced, the lonely man at their table kept staring at him.

When that man's name, Salim Sultan (1962), was announced, Anul Shetty could not resist coming up to his side of the table. He shook his hand and introduced himself. Both men stood and tried to remember each other. Some small talk to jog their memories led to the names of common friends and teachers. Then they embraced, and Anul Shetty invited Salim Sultan to sit next to him. Anul quickly introduced him to his daughter, Manesh, who keenly watched the two of them.

It was quickly established that Anul, a Hindu, was a couple of years older than Salim, who was a Muslim. Both of them were widowers. Anul lived with his daughter, Manesh, who was recently divorced and had no kids. Salim lived alone.

"*So, Salim, how far do you live from here?*"

"*Oh, not too far, about half an hour's drive.*"

"*Man, the more I talk to you, the more I remember things. You remember that drill teacher we had, Mr. Mukesh? Oh, my goodness, remember how strict he was?*"

"*How can I forget him? I was a victim of his cane beatings on my palms many times.*"

"*Oh, you too? Man, he was something. I don't know how those teachers got away with all that.*"

"*Times were different back then. I am sure they couldn't do that now.*"

Manesh sat quietly, listening to these old guys enjoying their talk about old times.

Then the time came to talk about personal stuff. Anul let Salim know that his wife of fifty-three years had died of cancer about two years ago. Salim noticed that Anul's whole persona changed. He looked at Manesh, whose sympathetic eyes were trying to comfort him. It was quite obvious to Salim how painful it was for Anul to even mention it. Anul then started talking about how much Manesh had sacrificed during that whole affair. He was blunt in saying that because she loved her parents so much, she'd sacrificed her own marriage. Her husband got sick and tired of Manesh giving all her attention to her parents and not to him. Manesh kept shaking her head, indicating to Salim that he should not listen to her dad.

Salim quickly brought the subject to himself, letting them know that his wife had died in a tragic car accident almost twenty-five years ago. He had been married for about fifteen years, and they'd had no kids. To insert some jest in the conversation, he added, *"That I know of."* All three had a laugh, and Salim was successful in changing the tone of the conversation.

They kept talking during dinner about different subjects, and Manesh could tell how happy her dad was. She had not seen him so engaged and involved for a very long time.

When it was time to go home, Anul seemed sad that the time had gone by so quickly. He insisted that they drop off Salim instead of letting Salim get a cab. *"That way I will be able to have some more time with you."* Anul was quite honest and not bashful at all.

Salim couldn't help but notice how sincere this man was. Anul didn't have the slightest tinge of prejudice in him. Obviously he was a Hindu, but he showed so much affection toward a Muslim.

Anul's old driver, Mustafa, was waiting for them when they were ready to go home. Salim gave him instructions as to how to get to his place. Manesh sat in front with Mustafa, and the two old friends sat in the back.

When they arrived at Salim's house, Anul insisted in asking when he would see Salim next. *"I just want to know."*

Salim kept telling him, *"Anytime you want. Look, I am alone and single, and I enjoyed this evening as much as you did."*

"All right, then, it's settled. I will send Mustafa to bring you to our house at 10:00 a.m. You be ready. We will have breakfast together. Maryam makes great parathas and omelets. Is that okay, Manesh?"

"Sure, Pops, that sounds really good."

"If that's the case, who am I to muddy the water? I look forward to it," Salim responded.

"By the way, Maryam is Mustafa's wife, and they are like family. We have been together for over twenty years. They live adjacent to our house, inside the same compound. We all love Maryam's cooking."

"That's great. I can't tell you how happy you have made this lonely old man. I will see you all tomorrow."

"Salim, it's the other way around. You have made me extremely happy. Manesh will attest to it: I don't get excited about anything anymore."

Salim could see the back of Manesh's head nodding in agreement.

2

The next day, Mustafa was at Salim's door on time to pick him up. Salim was ready and anxious to see his new friend again. Salim thanked Mustafa for picking him up so early in the morning.

"*Oh, come on, Salim Sahib. It is due to you that Babu Sahib*"—he called Anul by that name as a sign of respect—"*has been so happy. This is the least I can do.*"

As soon as Salim got to the house, Anul and Manesh were at the door, welcoming him profusely. Salim was overwhelmed with their warmth and kindness.

"*I am ready for some parathas,*" Salim declared. All four of them took a seat at the dining table, Maryam was introduced to Salim, and they enjoyed their breakfast with traditional Indian tea.

Salim complimented Maryam's cooking repeatedly and told Anul how right he was about the great breakfast.

After breakfast, everybody went their separate ways, leaving the two old guys alone to enjoy each other's company.

Anul told Salim about how he'd started out his career as a young clerk in a life insurance company and worked his way up until he retired as an executive vice president. Manesh was his only daughter, and he and his late wife had poured all the love they could muster into their only child.

"*Well, I can see that. And now you are bearing the fruit! Look at how she is giving back the love you gave her.*"

"*I know. I cannot tell you how it distressed me when it was affecting her marriage. I tell you, her ex-husband, Sunil, was not a bad person. But how much could the poor husband tolerate? No matter how much I tried to make her understand, she wouldn't listen. Sunil was very patient and gentle with her* for a long time, but it was bound to happen. Now it's just the two of us with Mustafa and Maryam."

Salim didn't say anything, but he admired the bond between father and daughter.

"*So, Salim, what about you? How has it been for you? What were you doing before you retired?*"

"*Well, Anul, my life has been a little different than yours. I married late, when I was in my thirties. I was having too much fun before that. Then when I got serious about life, I helped my father run his own furniture company.*

"*Unfortunately, my wife passed away almost twenty-five years ago in a tragic car accident. I never remarried and have been single ever since. I am so used to living by myself. I have a housekeeper, Zainub. She is very nice and takes care of all my needs, and I am happy. Maybe happy is the wrong word. Let's just say I am content with my life.*"

"*Well, let's see whether we can change some of that,*" Anul said, surprising Salim.

"*What do you mean?*"

"*I mean, why would you want to live alone at our age, in a big house like that? I saw your house from the outside. You can live with us! We have plenty of rooms—and more importantly, warm hearts. I can't tell you how happy that would make all of us.*"

"*It's very nice of you, Anul, but I like being alone and am used to it. Besides, we have just met. Maybe you will start feeling differently after a while.*"

"*Salim, I can understand your hesitation. I can also understand you are used to being alone. But please don't question my sincerity. Once I commit to something, that doesn't ever change. With us old folks, our word is all we have.*"

"*I am sorry, Anul. I didn't mean to offend you in any way. That's the last thing I want to do, with somebody that I was so lucky to meet and whose friendship has become so precious to me so fast. I promise you I will think about it.*"

Anul was happy to hear Salim say that he would think about it. That seemed to satisfy him. "*Salim, you don't want to see an old man cry, do you*?"

Salim wanted to change the subject, so he asked Anul whether he played chess.

"*Oh, I love to play chess. Wow, that's another thing we have in common.*" He excitedly shouted for Maryam and asked her to bring the chessboard.

Maryam brought in a table for them that had rollers underneath, and she brought out a huge marble chessboard, as well as a box that had a beautiful set of crystal black and white pieces.

Salim was impressed. "*Oh, boy, this is a beautiful set. I can tell we will have a serious game.*"

"*You bet. I won't be so nice with you when it comes to playing chess. You'd better bring your best game!*" Anul joked.

The two old men became serious and got going. Both were determined to not let the other have the upper hand. One game went on for two hours. Both were patient, competitive, and stubborn until Manesh and Maryam came together to check up on them, wanting to know about lunch. The men were intensely involved before the women interrupted them.

"Well, what do you think? Shall we call it a draw?" asked Salim.

"Yeah, I agree. Let's call it a draw—this time. I will get you the next time!" said Anul.

Both of them laughed and seemed content with the result.

Manesh had sent Mustafa to run some errands, and Maryam had finished cooking. Everybody had lunch and afternoon tea. Manesh was so happy to see her dad in such a good mood.

Anul announced after lunch that Salim had promised to think about moving in with them, which brought a smile to the group's faces. They all wanted to see Anul continue to be happy, and they knew that Salim could be the source of that happiness.

3

After almost three months, Salim had enough of going back and forth between his own house and Anul's. He had made enough excuses and did not have enough stomach to delay the inevitable any longer. The two men had gotten so close that sometimes they would count the hours before they were together again. The intense insistence of Anul and Manesh didn't cool down any, and Salim gave up.

Salim's housekeeper, Zainub, had mentioned retirement several times. She wanted to go back to her village and retire there with her children and grandkids.

Anul had a large, luxurious house, and Salim adjusted in the new house in no time. In the last few months, he had slept over at Anul's house often, so it wasn't too big of an adjustment.

It was now a three-person family unit, and they had a tremendous amount of love to give to each other.

All three of them were secular-minded people. They would discuss everything that came to anybody's mind. Sometimes the subject of religion would come up. They would explain to each other the basics and the core meaning of each other's faiths, although none of them practiced their religion with any consistency.

One day Manesh asked Salim what he thought about all the terrorist activities going on around the world. She indicated how most of the time, some Muslims were involved. Anul tried to nudge Manesh without saying that it may not be an appropriate question and that Salim might get offended.

Salim let them know that he was not offended and was okay with it. "*Look, we are like a family. We should never hesitate to ask each other anything.*"

After he said that, it put the two of them at ease.

"*To answer your question, there are some Muslims who*

have been brainwashed by religious fanatics, sometimes even by imams and religious experts. These are mostly vulnerable, uneducated, unemployed, and underprivileged people. It is always easy to manipulate the thinking of uneducated and ignorant people. Sometimes they are told that the world is out to get them because they are Muslims. Sometimes they are told that it is okay to harm and terrorize non-Muslims because they are sinners and kafirs, or infidels. Sometimes they are incentivized and compensated for their acts. Sometimes they are told that they are going to go to heaven if they lose their lives. The poor guys fall for one of those manipulations."

Salim went on. *"As you know, there are all kinds of people everywhere, in all religions, among all nationalities. There are peace-loving people, and there are troublemakers. "I personally believe that all religions teach you to become good human beings. One should not interfere or make judgments about other faiths. Anyone who follows a certain faith should be able to do so because he or she believes in it."*

Manesh and Anul agreed by nodding while Salim was talking.

Although Mustafa was a loyal employee of Anul's and was very protective of the family, sometimes he wondered about Salim's faith. In his own mind, it bothered him that although Salim had a Muslim name and called himself a Muslim, he didn't act like one. He never prayed, never read the Quran, and never went to the mosque. As a practicing Muslim, it bothered Mustafa so much that one day he decided to do something. He told the imam at the nearby mosque what was bothering him. The imam promised that he would send some guys to talk to Salim.

Mustafa was afraid that Anul and Manesh might not like it if the strangers came to their house preaching religion. He told the imam when to send the preachers. In his mind, he decided he would inform the imam when Salim was alone in the house.

He also convinced himself that he was doing the right thing, trying to get a fellow Muslim to follow the right path.

About two weeks later, Manesh wanted Mustafa to take her to her friend Rahilla's house, after which she was to going to go shopping with Rahilla. Mustafa knew that Anul took a nap between 2:00 and 4:00 p.m. He told the imam to send the preachers around 3:00, and he warned Maryam to not tell anyone.

Around 3:00 p.m., there was a knock on the door. When Maryam opened the door, there were three bearded guys, one wearing the Arabic juba long shirt and the other two in ordinary clothes. They asked for Salim. Maryam went inside and told Salim there were some people at the door asking for him. Salim was surprised because he wasn't expecting anyone. When he went to see who they were, he was more surprised.

"Are you Salim?"

"Yes. Who are you guys? What can I do for you?"

"Brother, we are here to talk to you for a few minutes."

"Okay, sure, go ahead. Would you like to come inside? Who sent you here? How do you know my name? This is not even my house."

They came inside, and Salim took them to the living room, asking Maryam to make some tea for them.

The man wearing juba was their leader, and he started talking. *"Brother, we have come here to bring you to the right path of Islam."*

Salim was shocked for him to start the conversation in such a way. *"How do you know I am on the wrong path, and who are you to judge that?"*

"Well, we never see you at the mosque. You are living with kafirs. At this age, you should be worried about doing good deeds on earth. It's never too late."

Salim got upset when he heard that, and he asked them to leave.

The leader said, *"Wait a minute. I am telling you this for your own good."*

Salim got even angrier. *"You'd better get out, or I will call the police."*

The men stood up, ready to leave. The leader told Salim, *"You'd better watch out. We know where we can find you, you old man, you kafir."*

By this time, Salim was shaking with anger. He didn't know who they were, who had sent them, how they had found out where he lived, and what their future intentions were.

Mustafa and Manesh came back in the evening. Salim decided to not tell Manesh and Anul what had happened because he didn't want them to worry. He asked Maryam to not say anything to anyone.

Maryam did tell Mustafa what had happened because she had been listening from the other room. Mustafa was shocked. His understanding was that the imam would send some people to talk, not to threaten him. He regretted what he had done but couldn't do anything about it.

The next time Mustafa went to the mosque, he told the imam what had happened. The imam told Mustafa that Salim was a lost cause, and it was okay to put some fear in his heart.

Mustafa disagreed.

4

Like everything else in life, things didn't stay the same. It had been almost two years since Salim had moved in with Anul and Manesh. Everything was going well until Manesh noticed something about her dad.

Ever since Salim had moved in, they had started playing a sort of a game among the five people who had meals together in the household. They would take turns in picking a dish each day of the week for Maryam to cook. Each person would have a turn, and that person would request something different for lunch and dinner when it was his or her turn. The game was something different, and it broke the monotony and made things interesting for everybody, including Maryam.

Manesh noticed that Anul would sometimes request the same dish for dinner which he had already requested it for lunch. At first everybody laughed it off, but then they realized that it was no laughing matter. Slowly Anul started to forget other little things, then events, and then names of close friends and relatives.

Manesh and Salim were concerned when it got worse. They took Anul to the doctor to see whether it was something serious. The doctor informed them it was a mild form of dementia. Manesh did some research and was devastated to find out that this condition had no cure, and things were expected to deteriorate with time.

As expected, Anul's condition did deteriorate. He started to become cranky and irritable on top of being forgetful. Soon he was a totally different person.

Manesh and Salim attended to all his needs, sometimes taking turns at night. Anul had some good days and some not-so-good days. He himself knew that his time was coming closer. At times, he would look at Manesh with a worried look in his eyes, as if he were saying, *"What will happen to you, my child, when I am gone?"*

At times Anul would look into Salim's eyes as if he were saying, *"Please take care of my baby after I am gone."*

Salim understood that, and he would say "Anul, don't worry. I will always be there for her."

This went on for almost two years, and they tried their best to prolong his comfort as much as they humanly could until Anul gave up.

5

Salim and Manesh were now living in the house by themselves. Both of them were overwhelmed with grief and grieved in their own ways. Together, they would console each other all day, and then they would separate and go to their own rooms at night.

Although there was a huge difference in age between them, they had different religious affiliations, the house was huge, and their bedrooms were far apart from each other, still the rumor mill started. The culture looked suspiciously at a man and a woman living together.

At times, Manesh would not let go of Salim. She would not want to go to sleep, and she accused him of being a coward when he tried to leave to sleep in his own room.

She would say things like, *"I don't care about age. Age is just a number. What is it that is bothering you? My religion? We are both nonreligious people; I don't go to the temple, and you don't go to the mosque. Are you worried about what people are going to say? You told me a million times that you don't care about what people think, so were you lying to me then? If you really loved your friend as much as I loved my father, then all you should care about is how happy his soul is going to be that the two people he loved the most are together and taking care of each other. That's all that you should care about, and that's all that should matter."*

Salim was confused, but under no circumstances would he entertain the thought of leaving Manesh. Besides, he had given his word to his best friend and soulmate that he would always take care of her and be with her. His best hope was that with time, the hurt and the pain would subside.

He even contacted Sunil, her ex-husband, who was sympathetic.

Manesh didn't want any part of it. At times, Salim would see and hear Manesh talking to herself as if she were having a conversation with Anul and pretending her father was listening to her.

Anul's friends periodically called to check on how Manesh was doing, as well as to show their sympathy and concern. One of Manesh's best friends, Rahilla, often called, visited, tried to entertain her, and tried to take her to the movies or shopping, but Manesh was simply not interested.

One day, one such call came from their bank manager, Mr. Sharma, who wanted her to come to the bank to sign some documents.

Manesh was in no mood for such chores and hassles at that time. She requested Salim take care of it, letting Mr. Sharma know that she fully trusted Salim, who was like family.

Mr. Sharma was not only Anul's banker but was also a family friend. He had already known about Salim's status with the family. Mr. Sharma took Salim out for lunch and wanted to get to know him better. Salim let Sharma know how hard it was for Manesh to absorb the jolt of her father's death and how distraught she was. Sharma had already figured it out by talking to her on the phone.

Sharma asked Salim whether he could bring Manesh to a get-together he was having at his house. He thought it would help get her mind off of things at home. Salim was skeptical she would agree, but he promised to try because it would be good for her.

Manesh agreed to go to Mr. Sharma's party at Salim's insistence.

6

The party was more elaborate than Manesh and Salim had expected. Over a hundred people were in attendance. Sharma was busy introducing different guests.

Salim was shocked when Mr. Sharma introduced one particular couple to him and Manesh. The lady's name was Shagufta, a name Salim would never forget in his life. Salim and Shagufta had had a short but intense fling before Salim's marriage. Although they both recognized each other, when introduced, they pretended otherwise because they were with other people.

Manesh didn't want to stay at the party for very long, and they left early—but not before Salim slipped a piece of paper in Shagufta's purse with his number on it.

Shagufta was one of the prettiest girls in Salim's school back in the day. Salim was popular and was the school hotshot for his athleticism and good looks. He knew that the girls were attracted to him. He used to bet with his friends that he could "conquer" any girl. Once the bet was won, he would move on. Shagufta was one of his victims. Although she knew that he had roving eyes, she still fell for him, hoping that he would find her to be special.

When he disappeared after getting her pregnant, she was extremely angry and disappointed, particularly in herself. She didn't know what to do. On the other hand, she felt very lucky to have found Dilip so quickly after the breakup with Salim.

Meeting with Salim at Mr. Sharma's after so many years was quite shocking. When she first found his phone number in her purse, she couldn't decide whether she should contact a man who had deceived her and left her. Then she thought about her son, who had been wondering about his biological father practically all his life.

Salim hadn't heard from Shagufta for two days, and he was getting anxious. Finally, she called. The first words that came out of her mouth were, "Salim, I really didn't think that I will ever see you again in my life, and I am still not sure whether I should even be talking to you. I am scared. I am a married woman, and if Dilip ever finds out, he will never forgive me—especially if he finds out about our history."

Salim didn't expect this kind of reaction from her, but he was old and experienced enough to handle it. "*Calm down, Shagufta. First of all, I promise you I will never tell this to anyone. Second, we were together for only two months, and that was umpteen years ago.*"

"*You mean you won't even tell your wife?*" Shagufta assumed that the woman with Salim at the party was his wife.

"*No, of course not. First of all, she is not my wife; she is my deceased friend's daughter. I am more like an uncle to her. Didn't you notice our age difference?*"

"*I don't know. Some people like to have young wives,*" Shagufta quipped.

Salim told her his whole life story, and Shagufta told him hers. They were both extremely interested in each other's history. Then there was a big pause.

7

Shagufta finally broke the silence. *"I want to tell you something. Salim. You'd better sit down. How's your heart condition? I hope it's not weak. I don't want to give you a heart attack."*

Salim was now puzzled. *"Please tell me, Shagufta. Don't torture me like this."* He suspected he was about to hear something serious. *"I can take it, and I am sitting down."*

"Okay, because you have promised you are not going to tell anyone, I will tell you. Soon after you disappeared from my life, I found out that I was pregnant. I looked for you everywhere, but you were nowhere to be found."

Salim was shocked to hear this. He'd had no clue. He obviously wanted to hear more.

"I have kept this secret from everyone, including my husband, Dilip. To this day, he thinks Ashok is his son. I never had any other children; he is my only one. His name is Ashok. Because his father, Dilip, is a Hindu, he was also raised as a Hindu. He lives in New York. He was married once for a short time, but now he is happy being single, and he has no children. By the way, Ashok and I have no secrets between us. I have told him everything about me and the disappearance of his biological father. Hopefully he has told me everything about himself."

Salim was so exasperated that he could barely breathe. *"Oh, my God, Shagufta. I don't know what to say, except that I cannot tell you how sorry I am for what I did and what you had to go through."*

Salim could tell Shagufta was trying very hard to try to conceal her emotions.

"Look, whatever happened, we cannot do anything about it now. I am with Dilip after all these years. He has been a good husband and an excellent father. I never want to hurt

his feelings. He was interested in me ever since he first saw me. My parents found out about my pregnancy, so when you disappeared, they quickly made arrangements, and we were married within a short time."

Salim told her that he understood, and he promised that he would never do anything to jeopardize their relationship. Then Salim asked her whether she was going to reveal all this to Ashok.

Shagufta didn't hesitate to answer that question. *"Absolutely. Like I told you, my son and I have no secrets. He will be thrilled to know the whereabouts of his biological father. He has been curious all his life about you. You see, all these years, we have been successful in keeping it from Dilip, so we have become experts. But I don't want to be overconfident and take things for granted. My dear Dilip is so innocent, probably because he loves both of us so much. He completely trusts us."*

Salim was overwhelmed with this new development that he quietly listened. As flabbergasted as he was, he didn't know what to say.

After they hung up, Salim went straight to his bed, quietly trying to digest what had just happened and trying to figure out whether this was a dream. It was only 6:00 p.m., and he was already in bed.

Manesh, who was looking for him all over the house, found him in bed at the unusual time and was concerned. She threw questions at him. *"Are you all right? What's the matter? I noticed you were on the phone for a long time. Everything okay? Why are you in bed at this time of the day?"*

"I am all right, just a little tired. Didn't sleep well last night. Maybe I should go to bed early and catch up on my sleep. I should be all right by tomorrow."

"Okay. Good night," Manesh said.

But of course, Salim could not sleep. While tossing and turning, he kept thinking about his son, Ashok. Not in his wildest dreams had he imagined this was how things would turn out.

All these years, he had been living alone and going through an ordinary and uneventful life. Then all of a sudden, he met his old friend Anul and quickly became unimaginably close to him. Then there was Manesh, then Shagufta, and now Ashok, his own flesh and blood.

"My God, what's next in store for me?" He kept wondering all night. "Is this a dream? A nightmare? Is this God's way of punishing me for all the sins I have committed?"

Shagufta's words kept ringing in his ears about how she was going to tell Ashok about his biological father and how thrilled he would be. Salim didn't know what he was going to say to Ashok if Ashok asked why Salim had abandoned his mother. He didn't know how he was going to break the news to Manesh. Too many unanswerable questions kept him up all night.

8

Salim got up in the morning with his phone ringing off the hook. He was half asleep, having not slept most of the night. The first words he heard from the other side when he answered the phone were, *"Hi, Dad."* He could not believe it. Those were the sweetest words he had ever heard in his life.

"Oh, my God. Ashok, are you for real?" he said while wiping his teary eyes. *"My son, my child, I wish I could see you, be with you, hug you."*

"Calm down, Dad. I don't want you to have a heart attack. Mom just gave me your number, and I immediately called you. Don't worry; I am going to come and see you as soon as I can. Believe me, I want to see you as much as you want to see me."

"That's not possible," replied Salim. *"I wasn't able to sleep all night, ever since Shagufta told me about you."*

Before they hung up, they both said *"I love you"* to each other, which was very unusual for Salim.

It had been a routine for Salim and Manesh to have meals together. At breakfast, Salim was unusually quiet with all the commotion in his head. Manesh sensed something was up but didn't want to make a big deal about it. Salim was determined to keep all the news from Manesh. He didn't think she would be able to handle all these changes well.

He could hardly wait to talk to Shagufta again and get some ideas about how to handle this unbelievable dilemma. He hoped that Shagufta would know more about how soon he would be able to see Ashok.

When the phone rang again, to his delight it was Shagufta. Manesh was not nearby. He was thrilled to hear from her.

"I know you have talked to Ashok. How do you feel?"

"Do you really have to ask? I am walking on clouds. I am in

heaven. I couldn't sleep all night, my appetite is gone, and I am an old man in my seventies. Does that answer your question?"

Shagufta laughed hard. "*Settle down, old man. That's a small price you are paying for the mess you have created,*" she joked.

"*Shagufta, seriously, how does Ashok feel? What did he say?*" Salim was anxious to find out.

"*Oh, he was just as excited as you are. I can hardly wait to see you two together.*"

"*How often does he come to see you and Dilip?*"

"*He comes once a year, and we go to America every other year. It's been like this for a number of years.*"

"*How nice. I have never been to America. Maybe now he will show me where he lives.*"

"*I have no doubt that he would like you to visit him.*"

"*I heard it has become very difficult to get a visa for America.*"

"*Not for visiting your son. He is an American citizen and has been there for twenty years.*"

"*That's good to hear. I would do anything to be with my son. Did he give you any idea as to when he will be able to get away from work to come here?*"

"*Salim, he is a director in a big real estate company, so it won't be difficult for him to take off any time. But I am sure he will have to meet his prior commitments. I am guessing a week to ten days.*"

"*Wow, that's great to hear that he has some privileges.*"

He heard some footsteps, and he let Shagufta know he had to go. He saw Manesh coming toward him.

"*I feel like doing something different today. Are you up to it?*" Manesh asked Salim. She seemed to be in a good mood.

Salim almost always agreed to do whatever Manesh wanted. He always tried to keep her happy and tried to be considerate, subconsciously filling a fatherly role.

Manesh knew it, and she knew Salim genuinely cared for her. She was appreciative without actually saying it.

24

"How about a long drive somewhere? That will take our minds off of things," Manesh suggested.

"Sure. Where would you like to go? Do you want to let Mustafa know, or do you want me to tell him?" Salim asked.

"I will tell him; you go get ready."

As soon as Manesh turned around to inform Mustafa, Salim made a quick phone call to Shagufta, to let her know about his plans, and told her that he would call her the next day.

9

Salim was glad to find Manesh wanted to do something different. She was coming out of her shell by agreeing to go to Mr. Sharma's party and wanting to go for a long drive, which meant that he was right about being patient with her and giving her some time to heal.

Mustafa was cheerful as usual, and Manesh brought along some snacks. It was a great day outside, not too hot or muggy.

Mustafa, upon seeing Mame Saab (Madam) in a good mood after a long time, even took the liberty of putting on some of her favorite music without asking her. He looked in the rearview mirror to get her approval, and she gave him a smiling nod.

They were off to a lake near Delhi that Manesh had heard about, called Damdama Lake. It was about three hours' drive. Everybody was happy to get out of town, and it was the first time they were going somewhere for a picnic since Anul's passing.

It was a great scenic drive. Mustafa was an old hand at this and made sure to drive slowly at certain points so everyone could soak in the scenic areas. The breathtaking scenery captivated everyone. There were long, curvy, narrow roads along the way, which made Mustafa's job more challenging but fun.

They got to the lake at a decent time. The sun was shining brilliantly, and the water in the lake glittered invitingly. Palm trees swayed gently in the breeze of the warm tropical sunshine.

They were able to spend several hours there. They enjoyed walking, playing cards, watching people, munching on snacks, and more before it was time to head back home.

It was already getting a little dark before they packed to head back home. All three of them had a good time. Although Mustafa was considered a family member because he had been with Anul for over twenty years, he always remembered his place. He never took their kindness for granted or tried to take advantage of their generosity.

While going home, Mustafa decided to take the same path by which they came because he was already familiar with all the roads. The roads were mostly one-way and curvy. As always with the one-way roads, some drivers were slow and careful, whereas others were impatient and in a hurry. Those drivers were ignorant of the fact that their impatience could be very dangerous for the responsible drivers. The impatient drivers always wanted to overtake the slow drivers regardless of the narrowness of the roads and traffic.

Everything was going fine, although the traffic was stop-and-go for three-quarters of the way. Suddenly this car behind them clipped their car in the left rear, impatiently wanting to overtake. Mustafa mistakenly thought he had some room on his right to let him pass, but he didn't. There was a ditch on his right behind the shrubs, and their car rolled over and fell into the ditch.

Manesh screamed in distress at the top of her lungs while holding on to Salim. The car went out of control. Fortunately, the ditch was not too deep, but the car had rolled over, and all three of them were a mess.

Salim was not moving, Mustafa had blood all over him but was still conscious, and Manesh was clinging to Salim, crying, and screaming about what they were going to do in this deserted area. It was dark, and there was no one around to ask for help. She could barely move herself. The car was upside down. She tried very hard to open one of the doors enough for one person to get out, and she succeeded. Somehow, she slowly took out her cell phone from her purse, not knowing whether she even had any signal in that area, and called 112 for an emergency ambulance. Miraculously, there was a response.

"*Hello, what's your emergency?*"

Manesh got some strength from nowhere. "*We have gotten*

into a car accident while coming from Damdama Lake. We
need help. Please hurry—our car has fallen into a ditch, and
my uncle is unconscious."

"Can you tell us your location?" Manesh didn't know. She
needed Mustafa's help, but he was still inside the upside-down
car and in bad shape, although conscious. She explained the
situation to the emergency officer.

He advised her to somehow handover the phone to Mustafa,
using the same door she'd used to get out of the car. "We will
try to understand him, no matter how incoherent he is. It will
give us some idea as to your location."

Manesh did as she was told. Mustafa was unbelievable:
despite multiple fractures on his face and neck, he was able to
let the officer know the proximity of the location. The officer told
Mustafa to let Manesh know they were sending a helicopter to
take them to the nearest hospital.

Miraculously, they heard the sound of a helicopter within
half an hour.

Within no time, they took everybody out of the car and took
them to St. Martin's emergency hospital.

At the hospital, they found out that Salim was in a coma,
with head injuries and a broken leg. Mustafa was also severely
injured, although all his wounds were treatable and not life-
threatening. Manesh's injuries were the least severe, but the
accident was very traumatic for her.

Manesh was obviously very worried about Salim, not
knowing when (or if) he would come out of the coma. After her
dad, he was closest person to her.

When Shagufta didn't hear from Salim the next day as
he had promised, she got a little concerned. She knew how
excited he'd been the day before, so it was puzzling for her to
not get a call. It was more puzzling that Salim's phone was dead
when she tried to call him. She called Ashok to let him know.

Ashok told her that he was also trying to call his dad, and
there was no answer.

When they couldn't reach Salim for another two days, they knew that there was something terribly wrong. Shagufta did not have Manesh's number and had met her only once, at Mr. Sharma's party.

Shagufta had no doubt by now that Salim was in some kind of serious trouble. She didn't want to call Mr. Sharma and ask him to call Manesh because that would raise a lot of questions; Mr. Sharma had only casually introduced them.

10

Finally, Shagufta decided to go see Mr. Sharma personally and talk to him face-to-face; the seriousness of the situation warranted it. She called him up, letting him know that she was coming to see him.

Shagufta's husband, Dilip, also had accounts in Mr. Sharma's bank for many years, and they had known each other quite well. It was always Dilip who had dealt with Mr. Sharma in the past, so this was a surprising first that Dilip's wife was coming to see him.

Shagufta was nervous and told him so. Mr. Sharma tried to calm her down, not knowing the purpose of her visit. Finally, Shagufta told him the reason for her coming to the bank.

Mr. Sharma was shocked at various levels. He too wanted to know whether Manesh and Salim were okay.

He called Manesh, who told him about the accident and the hospital where they were at. After several days, Salim had still not come out of the coma.

When Shagufta heard that, she was devastated. She was even more worried about how Ashok would take it. How would he react when he will heard about his father being in the hospital, comatose? He had just found out about who his father was.

She was also concerned whether Mr. Sharma was going to tell Dilip. What would he say? She was terrified that all her secrets that she had carefully protected for forty-five years were going to be exposed.

All these questions spun into her head at blazing speed. She thanked Mr. Sharma and quickly left. All she wanted to do at this point was go home, take some sleeping pills, and fall asleep, but she couldn't. She had to tell Ashok as soon as possible about his father's condition and which hospital he was in.

She told Ashok everything that Mr. Sharma had found out. She also told him to be prepared for the possibility of Dilip finding out everything.

Ashok was extremely distraught but wanted to be as supportive as possible for his mother, promising her he'd fly out there and be in India as soon as possible.

Dilip came home late at night. As soon as he came home, he went to the family room where Shagufta was watching TV.

"*What kind of a woman are you? Haven't I given you everything? I didn't know I had a snake living with me all these years. How am I going to ever trust you again? How am I going to believe anything that comes out of your mouth? Worst of all, my own son is somebody else's!*"

When Shagufta heard the last sentence, she jumped in. "*Please don't say that. You are the one who raised him. He will always think of you as his dad. You can blame me as much as you want; I won't even try to justify why I did what I did. But please don't blame Ashok—it's not his fault at all.*"

"*Don't try to be nicey-nicey with me now. All these years, he hid from me just like you did. He could have told me anytime. You must have so much influence on him. How can you make a pact like that among yourselves to keep it from me? I am supposedly the head of the household here, and I am the one who was kept in the dark. I didn't know anything! How can you do this to somebody who is feeding you and giving you shelter for all your life? Don't even try to come close to me. I will sleep in some other bedroom.*"

Shagufta cried all night. She had never seen this side of Dilip before, and she couldn't sleep until the wee hours of the morning. When she got up, Dilip had already gone to work without waking her or having breakfast.

Ashok called and let her know that he had succeeded in getting that evening's flight out.

She told Ashok how mad Dilip was, and they consoled each other. Both understood that the most crucial thing at the moment was Salim, whose life was in danger.

Ashok called Dilip. The first thing he said when Dilip answered the phone was, *"Dad, no matter what happens, my love for you will never diminish. I promise you that."*

Dilip was in no mood to talk; he simply listened.

"I am coming home by this evening's flight," Ashok added.

Dilip asked, *"Have you talked to your mom?"*

"Yes."

"Of course you have. Why did I even bother to ask?" Dilip quipped.

Ashok continued. *"Well, I know you are angry, Dad, so for now I simply want to let you know that she and I will go to the hospital straight from the airport because people are close to dying there. Goodbye for now, and I will see you soon."*

11

___

Ashok's delayed flight finally arrived at New Delhi Airport. Shagufta anxiously waited with her driver, Venu, for him to arrive. After the customs clearance, Shagufta embraced her son tightly and wouldn't let go of him while crying profusely.

Finally, they all sat in the car. Shagufta had already told Venu where the hospital was. She repeatedly instructed him to drive carefully.

After they arrived at the hospital, they met with the attending physician, Dr. Khanna. The doctor informed them that Salim was still in coma with a brain injury, and his knee was severely damaged. He was breathing on his own, and there was only a 25 percent chance for his survival.

Mustafa had a neck injury and would need neck braces for at least three months. Manesh was the least injured, and they could meet with her.

Ashok asked Dr. Khanna whether he could see Salim, and he asked how Salim's sense of hearing was, although he understood that the patient would not respond.

Dr. Khanna gave Ashok permission to see the patient and told him that he was not at a stage where he could hear anything.

While Ashok was escorted to Salim's room, he felt extremely nervous. He was about to see his dad for the first time in his life. He squeezed his mom's hand tightly. Shagufta was eager to see Ashok's reaction.

When they got to the room, Salim was lying there lifeless, in a vegetative state. Ashok ran toward him and hugged the lifeless body. *"Dad, my father, my father. I am here. Your son is here."* He kept saying that while weeping like a baby.

Shagufta also cried, not expecting Ashok's intense reaction.

Dr. Khanna watched all this from the other side of the bed

with an astonished look on his face, not quite understanding what was going on.

When Ashok took his head off his father's chest, his eyes were red like a tomato, and his nose and eyes were dripping. He didn't care about the doctor's reaction. The only thing he said to the doctor was, "*I am seeing my father after a long time, and I don't want to lose him.*"

Dr. Khanna patiently waited for them to finish and let them spend as much time as they wanted with Salim. When they were finished, he took them to his office.

Ashok realized how nice and considerate Dr. Khanna was, and he eventually gained enough confidence to tell him everything.

When the doctor found out that Ashok had just met his father for the first time in his life and had flown over twenty hours straight from America, he was flabbergasted. "*I must say, Mr. Ashok, I have been in practice almost thirty years, but I have never seen such a case. I can assure you that I will do everything I possibly can to monitor your dad's condition personally, and I will keep you updated.*"

Shagufta and Ashok profusely thanked him, knowing how important his role was going to be in Salim's well-being during the coming days.

The doctor said, "*Should I take you to visit the other two patients? They are both conscious and would be able to speak to you.*"

"Yes, of course," said Shagufta. *"But please don't tell them what we just told you about our relationship with Salim. They don't know it. We want them to know that we are just friends. We will tell them everything at the right time."*

The doctor was taken aback but promised to abide by their request.

Mustafa's room was on the same floor as Salim's, so they went to see him first. Mustafa was lying in the bed with a neck brace and bandages on his face. He couldn't move much. He had never met either one of them before. They told him they were Salim's friends and had come over to wish him well. Mustafa was very grateful.

12

The doctor took them to see Manesh. All her bandages had been removed, and she sat near the window, watching people come and go. When Dr. Khanna came to her room with two unexpected guests, she was pleasantly surprised. She recognized Shagufta, whom she had met at Mr. Sharma's party.

"Mr. Sharma told us about your accident. We want to wish you and Salim Sahib a quick recovery," Shagufta said.

Manesh was grateful yet slightly surprised, but she didn't say anything except to thank them.

Shagufta introduced them. *"Oh, this is my son, Ashok. He lives in America."*

They shook hands and acknowledged each other. *"I hope all three of you get well soon,"* Ashok said.

Shagufta and Ashok decided to stay at a nearby hotel, letting the doctor know they would come back the next day.

At the hotel, Ashok went to sleep right away because he was dead tired after the long flight and the drive to the hospital.

The next day at breakfast, Shagufta and Ashok got a chance to talk to each other face-to-face for the first time since all the chaos had broken out in the last few days.

Shagufta cried, questioning herself loudly whether all the decisions she had made in her life were the right ones. Ashok was quiet, which prompted her to ask him to say something.

"Ashok, this is not the time for you to remain quiet. I know you're my son, and usually parents give guidance and do not ask for it, but I am at a stage in my life where I can use some."

Ashok was close enough for him to give his mom a hug, after which he said, *"Mom, whatever you decide, I will always be with you. I have full confidence in you, and I know you will make the right decisions. You always do."*

Now it was Shagufta's turn to hug him. "*You have no idea how much it means to me to hear you say that.*"

After their private conversation, Shagufta called Venu and asked him to join them for breakfast before they went back to the hospital.

At the hospital, they directly went to Dr. Khanna's office, who escorted them to Salim's room.

Ashok again got emotional, but to a lesser degree. Then he asked Dr. Khanna a question that had been on his mind ever since he'd arrived. He asked the doctor whether it was feasible to take Salim to America and whether his chances of survival would improve.

Dr. Khanna thought about that question and responded to Ashok while looking at him in the eyes. "*Look, I hate to say this, but the more medical attention he gets, the better off he will be, and in India we are not even close to the advanced facilities they have in the States. He does have a brain injury, but it's not severe. Some patients come out of these types of comas after four to six weeks. He will also have to go through a knee surgery, but that surgery is far away in the process.*

"*One other important thing: you must know is that no action regarding him can be taken without Manesh's permission. You have told me a lot of things about your relationship with him, but they are all unofficial. All the official paperwork was filled out by Manesh, and she was fully conscious when all three of them were admitted to the hospital.*"

After a long pause, Dr. Khanna continued. "*My suggestion to you is to tell Manesh everything and try to persuade her that it will be in the patient's best interest to get his medical treatment continued in America. I will be happy to talk to her on your behalf, if you want me to, but you will have to go through your background story with her first.*"

Ashok looked at his mom, his eyes pleading for help as if they were saying, *Can you have a woman-to-woman talk with Manesh?*

Shagufta understood her son's dilemma, and she agreed to plead to Manesh on her son's behalf.

Dr. Khanna warned them that although Manesh appeared fine from the outside and didn't suffer any serious physical injuries, she had gone through a traumatic experience and might be going through post-traumatic stress disorder, better known as PTSD, so they would need to approach her sensitively.

Shagufta and Ashok decided to wait another day before approaching Manesh. They wanted to gather their thoughts and strategize how they would approach her. On their way to the hotel, they had to be careful in Venu's presence, but when they were alone, they started strategizing.

"Do you think I should be there with you when you talk to her, or would it better if it were just you and her?" Ashok asked his mom.

"Well, if it's just me, it would be less overwhelming for her, don't you think?"

"Yes, I agree. But do you think you can handle it? I mean, what would you say? How would you start?"

"It won't be easy regardless of whether you are there. At least with me alone, woman to woman, she won't feel threatened or uncomfortable by a man's presence."

"I hoped that by my being there, she might be more sympathetic toward me, knowing how I met my biological father, my own flesh and blood, for the first time and saw him in that state—and now I want to save him."

"I don't know how much Salim has told you about her, but from what I understand, they have become extremely close."

"Closer than me? I'm his only son, whom he abandoned."

"Don't say that, Ashok. He didn't know I was pregnant."

"I am sorry. I shouldn't have said that."

"What I was saying is that after her father passed, Salim is the only person she trusts for her well-being, and Salim is also very protective of her, like a daughter."

"Well, now he has a daughter and a son. Too bad he is in a

state where he cannot make such important decisions about his life." Ashok sighed. *"Mom, don't you think that if she really cares about him, she should see that he gets the best treatment, no matter where it is? Whether it's in India or America?"*

"I think if Salim goes away to America with you, she will feel abandoned with no one here."

"If that's the case, then it's pure selfishness. She will be thinking only about herself rather than what's in his best interest." Ashok seemed helpless.

The next day, they went to see Manesh. Ashok stayed in a hospital waiting room.

Dr. Khanna took Shagufta to Manesh's room. Manesh was sitting near the window as usual. When she saw Dr. Khanna and Shagufta again, she was a little surprised.

Dr. Khanna told Manesh that Shagufta was there to talk to her about something important. Now Manesh was really surprised, not expecting this in a hospital far away from home and under such circumstances. Dr. Khanna left the two women alone.

Shagufta started slowly. *"Look, Manesh. I am here to tell you something that you will be very surprised to hear, but please hear me out. I am sure that when you hear the complete story, you may not sympathize with me, but you will certainly understand it.*

"When we met at Mr. Sharma's party, it was not the first time that I had met Salim. We had met and known each other almost forty-five years ago."

Manesh's eyes popped up when she heard that. *"Oh, wow,"* was all that came out of her mouth.

"I never thought I would see him again. We had gotten very close during that time. I became pregnant with his child, and before I could tell him about my pregnancy, he had already moved on. He disappeared from the face of the earth, and I couldn't find him no matter how much I tried. The man you saw with me yesterday is his son."

This time, Manesh stood up, *"What? Are you serious? What are you talking about? How can it be? This is unbelievable."*

"Believe me, this is what happened. My parents found out about my pregnancy and married me off to the first boy who showed interest in me. That was Dilip. You saw him with me at Mr. Sharma's party. Since we met at the party, I have told Salim everything. Ashok and Salim had also been in touch— until Salim's accident."

"Yes, I did notice Salim acting strangely the last few days. He said he was not sleeping well. I am surprised he didn't tell me anything. So does your husband, Dilip, know that Ashok is not his son?"

"He just found out last week."

"What was his reaction? How did he take it?"

"Not very well. He is steaming mad at me, of course."

"It's so unfair to him."

"Yes, I agree."

"Did Ashok find out last week too?"

"No. I have never hidden anything from Ashok. He has known throughout his life that Dilip was not his biological father. In spite of the fact that he has known all along, he and Dilip have always had an excellent relationship. Dilip has been a great father and husband."

At this point, Shagufta felt that maybe she had softened Manesh enough to get to her point. *"So, Manesh, we were talking to Dr. Khanna, and Ashok asked him whether his father's chances of survival would be better if he were treated in America rather than in India."*

Manesh's ears perked up when she heard that, and before Shagufta could answer that question, she immediately said, *"No way."* She didn't even wait to find out what Dr. Khanna's answer was. *"You know, I hate America. We went there five years ago to visit my uncle. They treated my dad so badly that we both said we would never go back there again."*

43

"*Oh, no. What happened? Dilip and I go there every other year to visit Ashok in New York, and we've never had a problem.*"

"*Good for you. That one time was the first and last time for me.*"

"*But what actually happened? You must have had something really bad happen to feel that way about America. You know that everybody wants to go there. Which state did you go to, and how long did you stay?*"

"*Well, it was not just one thing. It was a disaster throughout. We went to California for about four weeks. First of all, they treated my dad really badly at the airport and were disrespectful. They had no regard for my elderly father.*

"*Then the hospitality we expected from my uncle and his American wife was not there. They both went to work every day, and we were stuck at home all day with nothing to do. We felt like we were in prison. They repeatedly told us to not cook because they were afraid we were so backward we would burn down their precious house. The neighbors were so unfriendly, and they always gave us dirty looks.*

"*When they did take us out sometimes, we were stuck in traffic for hours. Should I go on? My God. My dad and I were amazed as to how anyone can live like that.*"

Shagufta shook her head. She got more nervous as Manesh went on.

"*Dr. Khanna told Ashok that Salim's treatments can much improve in America. What do you think?*"

"*Over my dead body. I will never allow that. What kind of a doctor is he? We are supposed to be one of the top nations in the world, and he thinks Americans are better than us? Hell, no. And your son just got here, but already thinks he can dictate to us what we should and shouldn't do? Typical American mentality.*"

Shagufta stayed calm, although she was getting angrier by the minute. "*Look, my son never said anything; he is simply exploring all the possibilities and looking at all options. His main objective is to see what's in the best interest of everyone."*

"Oh, really? Everyone? I can guarantee you it didn't even cross his mind what will happen to me if Salim is no longer here. I have nobody except him."

Shagufta had had enough. She excused herself and quickly went to see Ashok in the waiting room, where he was waiting anxiously. The look on his mother's face was not very encouraging.

"Son, I have bad news for you. She is a very stubborn woman. She plainly told me that she will never let this happen." Then Shagufta told him everything Manesh had told her, including how firm she was and her reasons.

"Mom, how can she stop me from taking my own father to get better treatment? His life is in extreme danger. He is my flesh and blood, and she is only his friend's daughter."

"I was hoping that we can resolve this amicably, but it seems like we are going to have to go see a lawyer," Shagufta nervously suggested.

"Hell, I will do whatever it takes. Obviously I won't be able to get back to work on time, and it will be expensive, but so be it."

They wanted to let Dr. Khanna know what had happened before they headed home and took the next necessary steps.

Dr. Khanna was sympathetic, but told them that his hands were tied. He did tell them that he would keep them updated on Salim's condition.

When they got home, Dilip had already finished dinner. He gave a warm embrace to Ashok but was cold to Shagufta. Ashok told him everything that had happened at the hospital, and Dilip listened carefully. Ashok asked him whether he had any suggestions. Dilip also thought talking to a lawyer was the only option. He also suggested a couple of prominent lawyers.

13

Ashok got busy the next morning, calling his office in the United States, calling Indian lawyers, calling US hospitals, calling the US immigration office, and so on.

Shagufta tried to talk to Dilip and soothe him, but he wouldn't let her come near him.

The lawyers told Ashok that he had a strong case, but he would have to prove to the court that he was Salim's son. The birth certificate had Dilip's name as his father, and Salim was unable to testify. It would be Shagufta's words against Manesh's.

Salim had been living at Manesh's house for almost two years before the accident, whereas Shagufta had not seen him in the last forty-five years. Manesh's case would come across as much stronger than Shagufta's with the available circumstantial evidence.

One lawyer whom Ashok liked more than the others was particularly enthusiastic about taking the case, convincing Ashok that the circumstantial evidence was strong enough that the judge could be swayed away in Ashok's favor. The lawyer's name was Mr. Bhagwan. Ashok hired him and asked him to go ahead.

When Manesh was released from the hospital, the first thing she wanted to do was get a transfer of both patients from an emergency hospital to a regular hospital that was not far from her house. That way she could move back to her own place and be with Maryam, who had not seen her husband since the accident and had talked to him only on the phone.

Manesh was not too happy with Dr. Khanna, who had made statements to Shagufta and Ashok that she didn't like.

She called Mr. Dharmendra, who was a family friend, and asked him for his help. Mr. Dharmendra was more than happy to help because Anul had helped him many times when he'd been alive.

Within a few days, the transfer of the hospital was finalized. Ashok and Shagufta were not informed. Ashok was later informed by Dr. Khanna when he called to check up on Salim.

It had been two weeks since the accident. Ashok pushed his lawyer to hurry up and file the case.

When the case was filed and Manesh got the papers, she was steaming mad. She thought her whole world was falling apart right before her eyes. First her father, then the accident, and now her only support, Salim, being snatched away from her by someone who didn't exist in his life until just a few days ago.

She had to hurry and hire a lawyer of her own, with the help of Mr. Dharmendra. They hired a well-known lawyer, Mr. Desai, who was famous for fighting for women's issues.

The judge gave both lawyers, Mr. Bhagwan and Mr. Desai, the option to choose whether to go to full trial and live with the consequences of that, or let the judge decide. The judge had a tremendous reputation for being fair, and after consultations with their clients, both lawyers decided to let the judge decide.

The lawyers presented their respective arguments before the judge. Mr. Bhagwan wanted the court to allow Salim to be taken to America and be treated there. Mr. Desai wanted the court to have Salim remain in India and continue his treatment within the country.

Mr. Bhagwan's arguments were as follows.

1. Ashok was the biological son and should have the right to decide what was best for his father. Manesh had no blood relationship with him.
2. Ashok had already been deprived of fatherly love all his life.
3. It was a well-known fact that the United States was the most technologically advanced country in the world, and Salim would get better treatment there. Salim deserved to be treated where his chances were the best.

4. That conclusion had been confirmed by the medical expertise of the attending physician, Dr. Khanna.
5. In America, Salim had a son, his own flesh and blood, who could look after him. Ashok had a successful career and was well established. In India, Salim had no blood relatives but just a single unmarried lady who did not have an apparent source of income.

Mr. Desai's arguments were as follows.
1. There was no proof that Ashok was his real son. The birth certificate had someone else's name on it. Ashok might be an imposter.
2. Manesh's house had been Salim's only residence for the last several years.
3. After Manesh's father had died, Salim had taken her father's place, and there were plenty of witnesses who could attest to the fact that he was just like a family member.
4. There was no guarantee that Salim would get good care provided to him if he came out of the coma. Americans were known to be harsh toward senior citizens, and Ashok would be at work. Most likely Salim would be in the hands of a housekeeper. The huge cultural differences between the two countries could not be ignored. In America, Salim would be dealing with so many unknown factors, whereas in India he would be looked after by someone who was like a family member and who would be with him all the time.
5. The patient's transportation so far away to a different country would be complicated in his condition, to say the least.
6. America was not an easy and friendly country to migrate to, and there could be many hurdles Salim would have to face.

All relevant parties appeared in court to witness the drama and hear the important decision that would affect their lives. Manesh, Mr. Desai, Maryam, Mr. Dharmendra, and Mustafa were on one side. Ashok, Shagufta, Dilip, Dr. Khanna, Mr. Bhagwan were on the other side.

The judge now had to decide after weighing the arguments of both sides. He wanted to take two weeks to give it a thorough review.

After two weeks, the judge made the decision. He decided that the patient could go to America. He said his decision was based purely on what was in the best interests of the patient.

The judge also said that although both parties had strong, legitimate arguments, he had to keep in mind the person who couldn't speak on his own behalf. He emphasized that if Salim came out of the coma, he must be asked about his preference. He must be asked whether he preferred to live in the United States or wanted to come back to India. That was the order of the court.

Ashok was thrilled about the decision from the court. Manesh was devastated and now had to completely overhaul her life. She must learn to live without her father or Salim.

14

Ashok used all his influence and resources to take Salim to America immediately after the judgment was rendered. Ashok got Salim admitted to one of the best hospitals in New York.

Dr. Elliot Goldberg was Salim's new physician. Ashok stayed in touch with Dr. Khanna in India and introduced him to Dr. Goldberg on the phone. Both doctors reviewed Salim's case thoroughly, and they came to the conclusion that his brain injury was not severe. For a patient who went into a coma, the first six weeks were very critical, and if the patient didn't come out of a coma in those six weeks, then the chances of revival were substantially decreased. It had already been four weeks for Salim; the next two weeks would be highly critical.

Ashok kept Shagufta informed. Shagufta was nice enough to keep Manesh in the loop despite what had happened in court. Although Manesh hated what had happened in the court, she still wanted to know how Salim was doing, and she was grateful to Shagufta for keeping her updated.

Miraculously, Salim slowly started gaining consciousness ten days after being admitted to the New York hospital. It was slow, but according to Dr. Goldberg, he was out of a life-threatening situation. Ashok was beyond happy, and he let Shagufta know as soon as he found out.

When Manesh got the good news, she was out of this world, jumping up and down like a little kid. She told Shagufta she didn't remember the last time she'd been this happy. She wanted to personally thank Ashok and got his New York number from Shagufta.

When Ashok heard from Manesh, it was quite unexpected. Shagufta had not told him about giving his number to Manesh.

Ashok thought Manesh would hate him for the rest of her life after what had happened in the court. At first he didn't even recognize her voice on the phone because he had talked to her only once at the hospital. When she told him who she was, he was pleasantly surprised.

"*I can't thank you enough for everything you have done, Ashok. I sincerely want to apologize for trying to stop you.*"

"*Thanks for calling, Manesh. I was worried that you would hate me for the rest of my life.*"

"*I did hate you for taking away the one and only person I care about.*"

They both chuckled.

"*Why do you love my dad so much*?" Ashok asked.

"*You see, I loved my dad more than you can imagine, and your dad and my dad were soulmates. Before my dad passed away after a long illness, he asked your dad to make certain promises, one of which was to never leave me. Of course, you were not in the picture then; otherwise, things would have been different.*"

"*Well, Manesh, he still has a long way to go before his recovery is complete. According to Dr. Goldberg, his consciousness is coming back slowly—and don't forget, after he is fully recovered, he still has to go through his knee operation.*"

"*One thing I know for sure now is that he is in good hands. Ashok, I have full confidence in you. I am so happy and relieved that he is with you.*"

"*Manesh, I really appreciate your saying that. Coming from you, it means a lot. I will certainly keep you abreast and will call you as often as I can. You and I both love him tremendously, and we both want the best for him.*"

Ashok called Shagufta after hanging up with Manesh. "*Mom, why didn't you tell me?*"

"*What didn't I tell you?*" Shagufta asked.

"*That you gave my number to Manesh.*"

"*Well, I just didn't. How did it go? Do I owe you an apology? Was she rude?*"

"*No, no. She was much nicer than I expected, giving me all kinds of compliments. I knew she and her dad had gotten close to my dad, but I didn't know the degree of bonding between all three of them."*

"Well, that's good, isn't it? Somebody else loves him besides you."

"Definitely."

Within two months, Salim had gained enough consciousness that he knew he was not in India. Ashok visited him every day. Salim's memory slowly came back. He started asking questions about how long he would have to stay in the hospital. Dr. Goldberg had suggested not operating on his knee for a few more months and letting him use a wheelchair.

Manesh was regularly in touch with Ashok. She could hardly wait until Salim was ready to talk to her on the phone.

Like a lightbulb turning on, one day Salim sat up from his bed when he saw Ashok. *"Where's Manesh? How is she? Why isn't she here?"*

Ashok tried to calm him down, softly laying him back on the bed. *"Dad, Manesh is fine. I talk to her all the time. We were waiting for you to get better. You can talk to her anytime you want."*

Ashok was worried that if they talked, the accident situation might come up, and that might adversely affect Salim's memory. He quickly called Dr. Goldberg, who told him to not worry.

Dr. Goldberg also told Ashok to not stop Salim from talking about anything he wanted or asking questions. Salim was fully conscious now, and stopping him would make him think that people around him were hiding things from him.

Ashok was relieved to hear that. He immediately dialed Manesh. It was about 4:00 a.m. in India, but he didn't care. Manesh picked up the phone, still half asleep. He immediately gave the phone to Salim when he heard her voice.

Salim said, *"Manesh, it's me. How come you are not here with me? How are Mustafa and Maryam? I can't believe it—I am talking to you!"*

Manesh wasn't sure whether it was real or whether she was

dreaming. *"Both Mustafa and Maryam are fine. I wish I was there with you. I hope to see you soon."*

She wasn't sure how much he was allowed to talk. She quickly wished him well and hung up, worried about overdoing it.

Salim then asked Ashok about Shagufta.

Ashok realized that his dad was going to ask him about everything. Ashok had made up his mind that he would tell him everything, whatever he asked. He remembered Dr. Goldberg's instructions to tell Salim whatever he wanted to know so that he didn't lose confidence in the people around him.

Ashok was curious about how much his dad remembered about the accident. He asked him questions regarding that and found that he remembered it in bits and pieces.

Ashok wasn't sure whether he should help Salim try to connect the dots or simply answer his questions honestly but only when asked a specific question.

Ashok slowly noticed that Salim's memory was coming back, and the old man connected the dots on his own.

Soon after, Salim was released from the hospital.

Ashok had already made arrangements for Salim in his house while anticipating his release. He had talked to his housekeeper, Roberta, who was a part-timer, about becoming a full-time employee. She was happy to do it. It was winter, and New York was freezing. Salim being in the wheelchair meant he had limited mobility.

Ashok had gone back to work full time. Salim and Manesh were now fully in touch with each other. Manesh had Mustafa and Maryam, whereas Salim lived with Ashok and Roberta.

Salim was happy that he had his son back, and he was grateful that Ashok was such a devoted son. Ashok was attentive to all his needs. In spite of all that, he terribly missed Manesh and India. He still missed Anul and remembered when he had repeatedly promised to him, *"I will always be there for her."*

15

Shagufta always thought about Ashok's well-being, especially now that she was basically alone in the big house; Dilip was all but ignoring her.

She was happy that her son had found his biological father and no longer felt a gap in his life. She made sure to keep emphasizing to Ashok that he should call Dilip and stay in touch with him just like before. Ashok was sensitive enough to understand that, and he never gave Dilip a chance to complain or feel differently.

She tried her best to get Dilip to forgive her, but there was no change of heart or progress there; the wound was too deep.

She frequently asked Ashok how he was getting along with Manesh. He was more and more impressed with her love and sincerity toward his father. Ashok couldn't believe how nonrelatives who had different belief systems could be so deeply bonded. He credited all that to Manesh's parents, who'd raised her that way.

Shagufta noticed Ashok's change of attitude toward Manesh, from initially not liking her to now throwing heaps of compliments toward her.

Although Ashok was very happy with Dr. Goldberg, who had been a tremendous help all across the board, Ashok had not forgotten Dr. Khanna, who had also been very helpful in India. He kept in touch with Dr. Khanna, respecting his opinions and seeking his advice. Dr. Khanna knew that Salim was in good hands medically, but he would always suggest to Ashok how to keep Salim busy and entertained. Ashok tried to take him out and see places in New York in spite of the bad weather and the wheelchair restrictions.

Like his mom, Ashok was a sensitive and caring person. He was always concerned about people around him and their needs. He was deeply into meditation and yoga, which taught him self-analysis.

He was aware that his dad didn't have much to do during the day while Ashok was at work. Salim was limited to watching television (mostly Indian channels), talking on the phone, and waiting for Ashok to come home. Roberta was from a different culture, and there was not much to talk about with her. Ashok was also fully aware of the fact that he was under a court order to ask his dad, when he was well enough, whether he wanted to go back to India.

16

Eventually, the day came that Ashok had been dreading. One day when he came home from work, Salim was waiting for him. Salim told him he wanted to talk to him about something important. Ashok immediately sensed it.

"You know how much I love you, Ashok, and how much I would hate to be away from you. But, Son, this is not a place for me. It just doesn't suit me. I am sure you know how much I have tried to adjust the last few months.

"Apart from all that, there's something else that is killing me inside. I can't stand the fact that after promising to Anul over and over again that I would always be there with Manesh, I am here and she is there. You know I am useless and can't help her in any way, but my presence in her life, being around her, is what matters."

He then added, *"Believe me, she doesn't say anything to me about coming back because she knows it will break your heart, but I can tell."*

"But, Dad, what about me? I will have nobody if you go back," Ashok pleaded.

"Son, I have just come into your life recently. I am sure you will have no problem going back to your life just like before. Besides, I will be just a phone call away."

"Yeah, Mom says the same thing, that she is just a phone call away."

"Think about it, Son. It pains me to have to make such a decision."

"But what about your knee surgery, which we have postponed? You don't want to be in a wheelchair any more than you have to, right?"

"Son, you decide about that. Pretty much everything is in your hands. God has been so kind to me by reconnecting me

with you. I don't know if I would even be alive without you, with all you have done for me."

"Dad, don't embarrass me. All my life, I did nothing for you, and now that I have a chance to be with you, you want to leave me," Ashok joked. *"I understand, Dad. America can be a lonely place sometimes, even for Americans. I will call Dr. Khanna and Dr. Goldberg tomorrow and discuss with them your knee operation."*

The next day when Ashok called the doctors, both were of the same opinion. The knee surgeries in India were just as common as in America, and it was not a complicated procedure.

Ashok knew that now he must do what was right. He would not be able to live with himself if he did not tell his dad that the court had mandated he ask his dad where he wanted to live, in America or in India.

He called his mom the next day. *"Mom, I have some news. Dad doesn't want to stay here anymore. He gets very lonely all day while I am at work, and I don't blame him. On top of that, his guilt that he has left Manesh alone, contrary to the promises he made to his friend Anul, is killing him. Although I am sad that he wants to leave me, I am so proud of him for the man he is."*

Shagufta couldn't resist some tears coming down her cheeks. *"And I am so proud of you. I know how much you want him to be with you and how hard you worked for him to get there. You are still willing to give up all that. Bless you for doing the right thing."*

"I have got your genes, Mom." Both chuckled. *"I have an idea. Can you do me a favor?"*

"Of course. Just name it."

"Let's surprise Manesh. I will tell Dad to not tell her anything on the phone. I will give you his flight information. You go with Venu and pick him up from the airport. Then take him to Manesh. I know she will be shocked to see him at her door unannounced, but that will be a lot of fun."

Shagufta liked the plan. "Okay, I will do it and let you know how it goes."

The next day, Ashok took a day off from work. Salim was happy to see him at the breakfast table; usually they eat breakfast together only on the weekends. Ashok let his dad know what the doctors had told him about the knee operation, and Ashok fully understood his father's desire to go back.

Salim opened his arms for Ashok to give him a hug. Both men had tears in their eyes. Roberta watched these grown men tearing up and tried to figure out what's going on.

Then Ashok told him about the plan he had made with his mom about showing up at Manesh's house unannounced. Salim also liked that idea and promised to not tell Manesh on the phone, although it would be a hard secret to keep.

Salim was to leave a week later. Ashok took the whole week off for them to be together. It was a very emotional week for both of them. They spent as much time together as possible, got up early, went to bed late, and did whatever they could do to stretch out the last few days.

They again cried at the airport. Salim reminded his son that he would only be a phone call away.

Shagufta did what she had to do according to the plan. She picked up Salim from the airport and took him to Manesh's house. When Manesh saw Salim, she almost fainted. At first she thought it was a dream. Then she realized that Ashok and Shagufta had hidden the plan from her and wanted to surprise her.

She was so grateful to Shagufta that she almost bent down to touch her feet. *"You are no less than an angel. You have no idea how much it means to me. I was all alone, and my life had become so unbearable and empty. I didn't know what to do with myself."*

"Manesh, I didn't do anything. It was Ashok's idea."
They all chuckled.
After having some snacks and tea, Shagufta and Venu left.

The whole house was full of renewed happiness and excitement, as if a long-lost family member had returned. Mustafa and Maryam couldn't conceal their emotions either. They were happy for Manesh, who always treated them as family members.

On one hand, Salim was happy that he was now with Manesh, where he belonged, and he wouldn't feel guilty of breaking his pledge to his soulmate. On the other hand, he had left his long-lost son to be by himself in a cold and foreign land, although he fully realized that it was his son's own choice to be there.

Manesh had dedicated a room in her house to keeping all of Anul's memorabilia, including his favorite marble chessboard table and the crystal chess pieces. There was a large portrait of Anul in the center of the wall with garlands around his neck. Manesh took Salim to that room. Salim loved it and kept looking at the portrait of his soulmate.

Then Manesh did something even stranger. She closed the door from inside and sat down next to Salim's wheelchair. She asked Salim to focus on the wall and Anul's portrait and started talking to the portrait.

"*My dearest Papa, you were right. You told me your soulmate would be back soon, and here he is. All your life, you took care of me, and you are still looking after me. I love you with all my heart, Papa, and will keep loving you until my last breath.*"

Salim got emotional at what he was watching, and then she told him what had happened in the last few days.

"*I saw him in my dream one week ago, and he told me that you would be back soon.*"

Salim told Manesh that he'd also seen Anul many times in his dreams, and Anul was always kind, gentle, and cheerful.

17

Manesh could hardly wait to thank Ashok for what he had done. She called him the first chance she got.

"Did you want to give me a heart attack?"

"No, I know you are a strong, young, and vibrant woman. I had no such fear."

"I didn't know people who live in America could be so nice. I am slowly changing my opinion about them."

"Slowly?"

"Yes, slowly, because opinions formed for such a long time cannot be changed quickly."

"Well, it didn't take too much time for me to change my opinion about you."

"Oh, really? What was your opinion about me—and how has it changed?"

"You really want to know? Honestly?"

"Of course I want to know, and I hope you are going to tell me honestly."

"If you insist, I will tell you. I thought you were a witch, and I really couldn't stand you. I thought you were this really wicked person who was standing between me and my dad. I had hoped to be with my dad for so many years, and one person wouldn't let this happen. I felt so helpless."

"Oh, my God," Manesh said. She didn't know what else to say.

"But I have to tell you, my mother always insisted that I put myself in your shoes and look at things from your point of view. My mother is such a great lady, and what she says always makes sense. She said that you were alone after your dad passed away and that my dad was like a third member of your family, so I was trying to take your only remaining family

member away from you. She also made me realize that in your part of the world, it wasn't easy for a woman to be alone."

"Your mother is an angel. I even told her that when I last saw her. Okay, so that was then. You said you have changed your opinion about me. What about now?"

"What I think about you now, I will tell you some other time." Ashok teased.

Manesh couldn't wait. *"Oh, no! Please don't do that. That's not fair! After all this, you can't keep me hanging like that. I won't be able to sleep. Please don't do this."*

"Okay, okay, I will tell you. Now, I think of you completely differently. You are a beautiful, caring, and sensitive person who has so much in common with me. We both care very much for the people who are close to us, and our attachment to them supersedes everything else. We both fight for the people close to us and do what's best for them, putting aside our own interests. How's that? Are you happy now?"

"Now you are going to make me cry." Manesh could not believe such compliments coming from Ashok.

"Well, you were able to make me say things that were deep in my heart. Not too many people can do that."

"You said I was beautiful. Did you mean that?"

"You are beautiful, inside and out. That's rare, and I don't say things I don't mean."

"That's quite a compliment coming from a handsome American boy."

"I am not a boy—I am four years older than you! My dad told me how old you are."

Manesh said, *"Oh, really? I wonder what else he told you about me?"*

"Lots of things. But I am not telling; I am a gentleman."

"Well, let me remind you, gentleman, that he is with me now, and I can ask him anything."

"Don't forget that I am only a phone call away."

"Ashok, seriously, would you ever consider living in India?"

"Well, why don't I ask you? Would you ever consider living in America?"

"That's not fair—I asked you first."

"No, seriously, if you come here, you, my dad, whom we both love so much, and I can live together happily ever after."

"Ashok, you asked me to be serious, so here is my serious answer. I am in my forties, and it will be very difficult for me to adjust to a completely different culture. I have been there, and I know how it is over there. Your dad will need to adjust too. Our love for him might not be enough. We don't want him to make so many adjustments at his age, do we? What will he and I do all day while you are at work? We'll have no friends or relatives, and there will be communication hurdles."

"Domestic help here is readily available. We are so used to Mustafa and Maryam. On the other hand, your coming here makes so much more sense. You will have Dilip here, your mom, your dad, and your childhood friend Gopal. India is your country, after all. Should I go on?"

"No, I think that's enough." Ashok chuckled. "Are you sure you are not a lawyer and haven't told me about it yet?" Then he continued. "Actually, I will consider it. I haven't yet, though. You are right: things are different now. Of all the people you mentioned, you forgot to mention one person."

"Who is that?"

"You."

"Me?" Manesh repeated.

"Yes, you. I don't know about you, but I have developed strong feelings for you."

"Oh, my God. Ashok, what are you saying? Have you gone mad? Do you want to make me cry again?"

"You can cry all you want, but I am putting it all out there. I can't help it."

Manesh couldn't resist. "Ashok, the feelings are mutual."

"Manesh, you have made me a happy man by saying

that. All my sadness about my dad leaving is now going to be bearable. I will have something to look forward to.”

“So you will seriously consider coming back to India? Is that a promise?

Ashok said, “*I haven't had these kinds of feelings for a long time. I thought that these feelings were dead and I would never experience them again. So how are we going to break this news to your mom and dad? Who is going to say what, and to whom?*”

Manesh replied, “*Well, you are the smart American one. You figure it out.*”

“*I don't claim to be smart, but I think I will break the news to my mom. You can tell Dad. What do you think?*”

“*Okay, that sounds good. I am getting nervous. You think your mom still likes me after all the problems I created for her beloved son? I am not worried about your dad.*”

“*I know for sure she adores you,*” Ashok assured Manesh.

“*What should I tell your dad? Can I tell him that you have promised me that you are coming back? Do I have your permission to say that? I am sure he is going to ask me when. What do I tell him?*”

“*Sweetheart, I don't have the answers to all those questions. Just tell him as soon as I wrap things up. Don't forget that I have lived here for almost twenty years.*”

Manesh loved it when he called her *sweetheart*. “*What did you just call me? Can you say it again, please*?” Manesh joked, “*You'd better get you used it, sweetheart.*”

“*Is that an American way?*”

“*No, it's a universal way.*”

Manesh could hardly wait to tell Salim the great news.

At first, Salim thought Manesh was so happy because he was back.

“*What is the one thing that can make you the happiest man in the world?*” Manesh asked Salim.

“*Well, I am already the happiest man in the world.*”

"No, even happier than you are now."

"I wish Anul were here so I could play chess with him again. That would make me very happy."

"Well, how about being related to Ashok? Would that make you happy?"

"Of course I would like to see him. It was hard to be separated from him, knowing that he is by himself in a cold country. I think it's a cold country weather wise, and the people there are cold. I already miss him, although it's been only a couple of days."

"Well, guess what? You won't have to be separated for too long."

"What? Come again? Repeat what you just said. What do you mean? Why did you say that? Are you kidding me? Is this another joke you kids are playing on me?" Salim was puzzled and shaken up. He even tried to get out of his wheelchair.

"Please calm down," Manesh said, gently pushing him back in his chair. She pulled out a chair and sat down next to him.

"This is one of the happiest days of my life, given what I am about to tell you. Ashok and I have gotten very close to each other. He has told me that he cannot live there while you, his mom, and Dilip, are here, and he misses India. He feels there's no longer any good reason for him to be there when all of you are here. He realizes at what age his dad is at. He has already lost so much time with you, and he doesn't want to lose any more time. Therefore he is going to wrap everything up and come back to India."

Manesh could see the stream of tears coming from his eyes.

"During my last days in New York, I did sense something, but I couldn't put my finger on what was going on. Of course, you never know what's going on in someone's head. The fact that he told you about all these important decisions and not me shows how highly he thinks of you in his life; that in itself is a very good sign. I can tell some higher power is looking after both of us."

Manesh nodded in agreement.

Ashok couldn't wait to tell his mom and get her reaction. Whenever he called her, the first thing he always asked was whether things had simmered down between her and Dilip. The answer was always, *"Things haven't changed, and Dilip's anger has not diminished."*

After the usual, Ashok said, *"Mom, I have something important to tell you. Are you sitting down?"*

Shagufta told him, *"This is my line. How come you are using my line on me? Yes, I am sitting down."*

"Because I am your son, and I have learned from the best."

"All right, all right. Flattery is not going to get you anywhere. What are you up to now? You almost gave Manesh a heart attack."

"Speaking of Manesh, I am calling to talk to you about her."

"What about her?"

"Well, I have fallen in love with her. How would you like to be her mother-in-law?"

"What? Are you serious? When did this happen? Have you thought it through? Very recently you had a strong dislike toward her. Are you sure?"

"Yes, Mom. I have given it a lot of thought. I like my life partner to be strong, genuine, sincere, and down-to-earth, and she is all that. Plus, she is Indian, and she is beautiful."

"Wow. Sometimes you don't know even your own flesh and blood, and how their thought process works. What about her dislike for America? How is she going to live in a country she dislikes so much?"

"Well, that's another thing I want to tell you about. You should definitely sit down."

"Ashok, what's the matter with you? Are you okay? Haven't you shocked me enough for one day?"

"Nope, I am not done yet. I have decided to come back home to India."

"Oh, my God, are you serious? What are you going to do

here? What about your career? Are you going to quit such a great job? Real estate is totally different here."

"Look, Mom. I have an MBA and have been in management for a long time. I can find something there. I want to spend time with Dad; he is pushing his seventies. I hope he lives for a long time, but one has to be realistic. Aren't you happy for me that I am coming back?"

"Of course I am, but once you are a parent, you are always a parent. You have to be cautious and look at things from all sides."

"So now can I talk to Dad?"

Shagufta put Dilip on the phone.

"Hi, Dad. How are you?"

"I am good. Good to hear your voice, Ashok. I heard Salim didn't like it in New York and came back."

"Yeah, he got lonely and didn't have much to do while I was at work."

"So what else is new?"

"Well, there is a lot I have to tell you."

"Oh, yeah? Tell me."

"I have two important things to tell you. First of all, I have decided to come back to India."

"Oh, really? That's great news! But why all of a sudden?"

"Well, because I am getting up there, and I want to settle down. I want to marry an Indian woman. I tried with an American once, and as you know, it didn't work out."

"Well, that's excellent news. We should probably start looking for someone suitable for you. I am sure Shagufta can find a perfect match for you."

"Dad, I have already found a perfect match."

"Oh, really? Who is that? Somebody we know?"

"Yeah. It's Manesh."

"What, are you serious? She is the person who fought so hard against you in court! Why her? You couldn't find anyone else in the whole world?"

"Oh, Dad, it's long story. She and I have been talking for a long time. We have much in common and have gotten very close."

"It's up to you, Son. Just be careful. I am sure you must have thought about it long and hard."

"Yes, I have. Now all I want is your blessing, Dad."

"You have my full blessing, Son."

Salim and Shagufta had not talked much since he had come back from America. Shagufta called him the day after they received the good news.

"Congratulations!" she said.

"You too," he said to her.

Both were delirious. Salim kept telling her that it was some higher power working, because his life had changed so much—and for the better. Shagufta teased him about never believing in any higher power in the past, but now his faith had come back.

Salim didn't have an answer, but he did mention that sometimes he wondered about Anul's spirit.

Shagufta initially dismissed his thoughts but was willing to listen to him out of politeness. Salim was convinced that the love between Anul and Manesh was so deep that even though Anul was not here physically, his spirit was restless whenever she was unhappy or insecure.

He himself felt relieved and calmed physically and emotionally ever since he got back to India. It was as if Anul were welcoming him home.

Salim said, *"I feel like when my child, Ashok, and Anul's child, Manesh, tie the knot and bond, in a way I will be bonded to Anul once again. Wouldn't that be wonderful? Then I can relax and die happy."*

In the meantime, Manesh passed by Salim and whispered in his ear, asking whether he was talking to Shagufta. He whispered back yes, asking her whether she wanted to talk to her.

She nodded. Salim told Shagufta, *"Guess who just walked by and wants to talk to you?"*

The two women started talking.

"Manesh, I am so happy. Ashok told me everything."

"Everything?"

"Yes, everything. My son and I don't keep anything from each other."

"I know. You are so lucky to have a son like him. Things are moving so fast. We both need your blessings."

"Well, don't you feel lucky too? You have Salim back in your life, and now Ashok. I hear you guys are talking up a storm."

"Yes, we do have a lot to talk about, a lot of catching up to do. I just need your blessing, and I hope that I will meet your expectations. I know I have done some unpleasant things in the past."

"Manesh, all of that is forgiven and forgotten. You did what you thought was the right thing to do. In fact, Ashok admires you for that. It shows your strength and how you can stand up for what you believe in."

Ashok was happy about the decisions he had made. Soon enough, he would be in his own country. He would be with his mom, his dad, his biological dad, and his future wife. He was in the real estate business, so it didn't take long for him to sell his house. Within three months, he was in India.

18

Everybody was there at the airport to greet Ashok. Somebody was leaving America to come back to India, which in itself was very unusual. Also, everybody genuinely liked him. Salim, Manesh, Mustafa, Maryam, Shagufta, Dilip, Gopal, and Venu were there. From the airport, they went to Ashok's house for a celebratory dinner.

Shagufta had prepared the dinner for everybody in anticipation of this happy occasion.

It was awkward for Salim to be at Shagufta's house. It was the first time Manesh had been at Ashok's house. Ashok was nervous about whether he had made the right decision.

Shagufta looked at Manesh as her daughter-in-law for the first time. Manesh looked at Shagufta as her mother-in-law for the first time.

Ashok was with two dads who were together for the first time. Ashok also noticed the distance between his dad and mom was still the same.

It was awkward for Dilip to have Salim at his house. This person was the cause of his whole life turning upside down.

But this was a festive occasion, and with Shagufta's hospitality, everything turned out fine.

Ashok was tired from the trip, so he excused himself and promised Salim and Manesh that he would come by in a couple of days. Salim wasn't satisfied by that and asked him to come by the next day. With Manesh nodding, and Ashok chuckled and promised that he would.

Soon after that, Salim, Manesh, Mustafa, and Maryam also left.

As soon as all the guests left and Ashok had gone to bed, Dilip screamed at Shagufta.

"*Who do you think you are? How dare you invite that man*

in my house without my permission! This time you've gone too far. You think you can do whatever the hell you want around here, and nobody will say anything!"

Shagufta had some inclination that Dilip might not like Salim being there, but she'd taken a chance, hoping that Dilip would be too happy about Ashok's return and would overlook it. *"I am sorry, Dilip. I didn't mean to upset you. It will never happen again."*

"It had better not. I can only take so much shit from you. Enough is enough. From now on, if you invite somebody to this house, you ask me first."

Shagufta had never talked back at Dilip, and she was not about to start now. She hoped that Ashok did not hear him shouting at her from the room next door.

The next day at the breakfast table, Ashok told his dad, with his mom present, that he had heard him screaming the night before. He didn't want his dad to feel that he was taking his mom's side. He told his mom that under the circumstances, she needed to be more sensitive to Dilip's feelings. He didn't want his mom to think that he was taking his dad's side, so he told his dad that Shagufta had invited Salim because she'd thought it would make Ashok happy. Ashok said that Dilip needed to put himself in the other person's shoes.

Ashok was able to pacify both sides. They both loved Ashok, and he was the most important person in their lives.

"Mom, Dad, I am happy to be here, and I am really glad with the decisions I have made. Now there is only one thing missing in my life."

They looked at him with puzzled looks on their faces.

Dilip said, *"What is it, Son? What can we do? What is it that you are missing? I will do anything, if it's within my power."*

"Really, Dad? You will? Promise?"

"Yes, I promise—if it's within my power."

"Dad, let me start by saying that you have been the best dad anyone can ask for. You have given me everything that any son can expect from his dad—and I don't mean material things, but

also emotionally. I will never forget that. Just because I have now found my biological father, that doesn't mean my feelings for you will ever diminish."

Ashok could see that his father was getting emotional. Dilip's eyes welled up.

"So coming back to what I am missing. You must have guessed it by now. Dad, you remember when I was a little boy? You used to tell me, 'Son, forgetting is not in your power, but forgiving is.' I have never forgotten that, and it is still true. Dad, I want you to forgive Mom for what happened. I know forgetting is not in your power, but forgiving is. Can you do that for my sake?"

Shagufta cried. She couldn't resist and said, *"Dilip, before you answer Ashok, I also want to say something. I agree with Ashok that not only have you been the best father, but you have also been the best husband. Although you have been angry the past few months, I know that you have a forgiving nature, and eventually you will forgive me. I wouldn't leave your side for a million years, no matter what."*

Now it was Dilip's turn. *"You guys, stop ganging up on me. When I first found out about this from Mr. Sharma, it was like somebody put a knife in me. I didn't expect this from somebody I was living with for over forty years. No one can imagine the hurt that it has caused me. It is a monumental task that you are asking me to do here, to forgive something of colossal proportion. I felt completely isolated in many ways. I thought my son was not my son. There was another man who was his father, and my wife's son was that man's son—so what did I have? Nothing.*

"Ashok, to prove how much I love you, and because I know how much you love your mother, I am willing to give it a try. It's not going to be easy, but I know how much it means to you."

Father and son got up and gave each other a big hug. Dilip motioned Shagufta to come up and join them. By this time, she was crying like a baby, but they were the tears of joy. All of them gave each other a group hug.

About the Author

Hanif Mike Karim emigrated from Pakistan to the United States in 1971. He was the National Table Tennis champion and No 1 player in the country for two years. He was also the Captain of the National Team that participated in the World Championship in Munich, Germany.

He has worked in the films such as *Two Brothers, The Holy Man, Drugs & Chocolates, Cerebrum* and *The Psychic*. He was the Executive producer, creator/writer and played multiple roles in *Two Brothers* which won several awards. He is currently Co-Producing a feature film based on his book "Where is Sophia", http://www.whereissophia.net/.

The title of the film is also the same "Where is Sophia", http://www.whereissophia.com.

He recently finished another book by the name of "Secular Soulmates", www.secularsoulmates.com. He did voice over work in Rambo III and has worked in theater as well.

He did his MBA in Los Angeles and retired from U.S federal government, where he worked in the law enforcement area for the Department of Justice.

He has his own website http://www.hanifkarim.com/.

He lives in the canyon area north of Los Angeles and enjoys writing, meditation, and biking. He has also returned to the table tennis circuit as a senior player. He is a former United States National Champion in the over 60 division.

Printed in the United States
By Bookmasters